I0441136

This Book Belongs To:

_____

BY
Home Planners And
Journals

This book is copyright protected.
Reproducing this book is prohibited
and not allowed without the
permission of the author. All rights
reserved.

www.ingramcontent.com/pod-product-compliance
Lightning Source LLC
Chambersburg PA
CBHW070104300526
45788CB00016B/2264